WRITERS' BRITAIN

ENGLISH POETS

In the same series

ENGLISH POETS

LORD DAVID CECIL

with
8 plates in colour
and
22 illustrations in
black & white

PRION

This edition published in Great Britain by Prion
32-34 Gordon House Road,
London NW5 1LP

First published in 1942 by Collins

A catalogue record of this book can be obtained
from the British Library

ISBN 1-85375-220-0

Typeset by York House Typographic Ltd, London
Colour origination by MRM Graphics, Singapore
Printed & bound in Singapore

I

EVERY GREAT NATION HAS EXPRESSED ITS SPIRIT IN ART: generally in some particular form of art. The Italians are famous for their painting, the Germans for their music, the Russians for their novels. England is distinguished for her poets. A few of these, Shakespeare, Milton, Byron, are acknowledged to be among the supreme poets of the world. But there are many others besides these. Shakespeare is only the greatest among an array of names. Seven or eight other English poets deserve world-wide fame: in addition to them, many others in every age have written at least one poem that has made them immortal. The greatness of English poetry has been astonishingly continuous. German music and Italian painting flourished, at most, for two hundred years. England has gone on producing great poets from the fourteenth century to to-day: there is nothing like it in the history of the arts.

That the English should have chosen poetry as the chief channel for their artistic talent is the result partly of their circumstances, partly of their temperament.

English is a poet's language. It is ideally suited for description or for the expression of emotion. It is flexible, it is varied, it has an enormous vocabulary; able to convey every subtle diverse shade, to make vivid before the mental eye any picture it wishes to conjure up. Moreover its very richness helps it to evoke those indefinite moods, those visionary flights of fancy of which so much of the material of poetry is composed. There is no better language in the world for touching the heart and setting the imagination aflame.

English poetry has taken full advantage of its possibilities. Circumstances have helped it. Nature placed England in the Gothic North, the region of magic and shadows, of elves and ghosts, and romantic legend. But from an early period she has been in touch with classic civilisation, with its culture, its sense of reality, its command of form. In consequence her poetry has got the best of two traditions. On the whole Nature has been a stronger influence than history. Most good English poets have been more Gothic than classical; inspired but unequal, memorable for their power to suggest atmosphere and their flashes of original beauty, rather than for their clear design, or their steady level of good writing. For the most part too, they write spontaneously, without reference to established rules of art. But they have often obeyed these rules, even when they were not conscious of them: and some, Milton and Chaucer for

The Distressed Poet – an engraving by William Hogarth, 1740.

instance, are as exact in form and taste as any Frenchman. No generalisation is uniformly true about English poetry. It spreads before us like a wild forest, a tangle of massive trees and luxuriantly-flowering branches, clamorous with bird song: but here and there art has cut a clearing in it and planted a delicate formal garden.

II

ROUGHLY SPEAKING ENGLISH POETRY DIVIDES ITSELF into four phases. The first, the medieval period, is a short one. During most of the Middle Ages neither language nor the laws of versification were sufficiently developed to be a vehicle for the best poetry. Only towards the middle of the fourteenth century were they ready. Even then, it is to be doubted if they would have revealed their possibilities without the genius of one man. Geoffrey Chaucer (1340–1400), the friend of Petrarch is the first great English poet; and he has remained one of the greatest. He was a story-teller. Of the two works for which he is remembered, the first, *Troilus and Criseyde*, re-tells a love romance about the siege of Troy; the second, the *Canterbury Tales*, is a collection of stories, serious and comic, supposed to be told by a troop of Pilgrims on their way to the Shrine of St. Thomas of Canterbury. Chaucer is a curious mixture of the old and the new. In his subject matter he looks back to that world of medieval Christendom which was approaching its end. His stories were old stories; legendary romances and popular anecdotes. And he tells them in the straight-forward spirit in which they were created. On the other hand his smooth easy style is something quite new; in his work we find the English language used for the first time to produce effects as delicate, artful and economical as those of the great writers of Greece and Rome. What is the life of man, he laments,

> Now with his love, now in the colde grave,
> Alone, withouten any company.

The sad fleetingness of mortal life, the solitude of death, is conveyed in thirteen words.

But Chaucer's mastery of style is only one of his gifts. He makes his stories enthralling, and his characters alive. The Canterbury Pilgrims, the fat, genial, gap-toothed wife of Bath, the gay young Squire, 'as fresh as is the month of May,' the brutal miller with his red scaly neck, are as vivid as people we have met. And he can trace with the subtle sympathy of a psychological novelist the guilty waverings of poor frail Criseyde. Indeed, of all his talents, it is his sympathetic spirit that most compels our admiration. Here again his spirit shows a curious mixture of old and new. Chaucer approaches life with the innocent zest of an earlier civilisation. He delights in spring flowers, in youthful beauty, in the

Geoffrey Chaucer (1345–1400).

animal humours of the body; a fresh gale, racy with the smell of earth, blows through his pages. But his attitude to life is not unsophisticated. He is a man of the world. He knows human nature well and has no illusions about it. Acuteness and charity combine in an ironical wisdom which sparkles over his pages in a silvery sunlight.

Chaucer left no followers to compare with himself. During the fifteenth century, medieval civilisation collapsed in a series of civil wars, and wars, as we know too well to-day, do not provide a favourable climate for poets. The only voices that made themselves heard above the storm were those of the anonymous, humble composers of popular ballads and carols. These however were enough to make the period memorable. The childlike sweetness of the carols, the wild lilt of the ballads, with their stark, tragic stories shrouded in an atmosphere of Gothic enchantment, disturbed the imagination and thrilled the heart with a direct sharpness, denied to most sophisticated poetry:

THE UNQUIET GRAVE

The wind doth blow to-day, my love,
And a few small drops of rain;
I never had but one true-love,
In cold grave she was lain.

I'll do as much for my true-love
As any young man may;

I'll sit and mourn all at her grave
For a twelvemonth and a day.

The twelvemonth and a day being up,
The dead began to speak;
'Oh who sits weeping on my grave
And will not let me sleep?'

''Tis I, my love, sits on your grave,
And will not let you sleep;
For I crave one kiss of your clay-cold lips,
And that is all I seek.'

'You crave one kiss of my clay-cold lips;
But my breath smells earthly strong;
If you have one kiss of my clay-cold lips,
Your time will not be long.

''Tis down in yonder garden green,
Love, where we used to walk,
The finest flower that ere was seen
Is wither'd to a stalk.

'The stalk is wither'd dry, my love,
So will our hearts decay;
So make yourself content, my love,
Till God calls you away.'

With the beginning of the sixteenth century, professional poetry began to raise its head again, led by the fantastic, playful Skelton and the graceful amorous verses, modelled on classic and Italian poetry, of Wyatt and Surrey. But it was not till the reign of Elizabeth, that it emerged into full sunlight. The world that met its eyes was a changed world. England had broken with the Catholic Church, had established a new triumphant monarchy, and was on the way to lay the foundation of an Empire. Her new-born vitality and self-confidence expressed itself in a tremendous outburst of poetic talent. For a hundred years England was alive with poets, lyric poets, dramatic poets, narrative poets, philosophic poets; and among them the greatest she ever produced. Their work reflects the age they lived in, the Renaissance; a multi-coloured age, cruel, fantastic and glorious, mingling in a bewildering complexity, horror and beauty, barbarism and subtlety.

It passed through two phases. The first, the early Renaissance, was hopeful and joyous. After the darkness of the preceding age, man rioted in his newly discovered sense of life's splendour. This poetry is sumptuous and musical in form, in mood it is ideal and magnificent. The chief figure among non-dramatic poets is Edmund Spenser (1552–1599). His great work, *The Faerie Queene*, is a long symphonic poem, in the form of a fairy-tale romance about knights and ladies, composed in celebration of Queen Elizabeth, and in praise of those

☙ Skelton Poeta. ☩

Et emo mansura die dum sidera fulgent
Equora dum qꝫ tument hec laurea nostra virebit
Hinc nostrum celebre et nomē referetur ad astra
Vndiqꝫ Skeltonis memorabitur altera donis

John Skelton (1460-1529).

noble qualities to which it should be the aim of her subjects to aspire. Still medieval in its feeling for the magical and the marvellous, it blends the idealism of chivalry, its belief in piety and heroism and poetic love, with a pagan delight in sensuous beauty. It is a strange mixture. Venus and King Arthur, the arch-angel Gabriel and Queen Elizabeth, jostle one another in an endless confusion of fabulous adventure. But this confusion is more than made up for by Spenser's poetic intensity. An iridescent glow of beauty suffuses his whole canvas, harmonising its most incongruous elements, and breathing forth its spirit in a stream of melody, honeyed, dreamy, and intricate; which lulls the critical mind to sleep, like a spell woven by one of the poem's own sorcerers.

SPENSER'S MARRIAGE

Open the temple gates unto my love,
Open them wide that she may enter in,
And all the posts adorn as doth behove,
And all the pillars deck with garlands trim,
For to receive this Saint with honour due,
That cometh in to you.
With trembling steps, and humble reverence,
She cometh in, before th'Almighty's view;
Of her ye virgins learn obedience,
When so ye come into those holy places,
To humble your proud faces:

Edmund Spenser (1552–1599).

Sir Walter Raleigh (1552-1618).

Bring her up to th'high altar, that she may
The sacred ceremonies there partake,
The which do endless matrimony make;
And let the roaring organs loudly play
The praises of the Lord in lively notes;
The whiles, with hollow throats,
The choristers the joyous anthem sing,
That all the woods may answer, and their echo ring.

From THE EPYTHALAMIUM

At the same time, a school of courtly poets arose – Sir Walter Raleigh and Sir Philip Sidney are the most famous of them – who expressed a similar spirit on a smaller scale. In mellifluous and flowered phrase, they carol of silken dalliance and Arcadian shepherds, of winged Cupid and the rose of pleasure that must be plucked ere it withers. In a sense, these poems are artificial productions; sentiment and imagery alike are conventional; in another sense they are as natural as the song of birds; spontaneous outpourings of youthful fancy, intoxicated by the loveliness of the world.

The fields breathe sweet, the daisies kiss our feet,
Young lovers meet, old wives a-sunning sit,
In every street these tunes our ears do greet –
Cuckoo, jug-jug, pu-we, to-witta-woo!
Spring, the sweet Spring!

From SPRING *by Thomas Nashe*

Christopher Marlowe (1564–93).

A similar intoxication permeates the other great literary form of the period, the drama. Otherwise it was very different, not courtly and formal, but haphazard, racy and popular. The Elizabethan theatre was, at its inception, a very humble affair, controlled by troops of vagabond mummers, who roamed about from inn to great house providing entertainment for any one they could attract to their performances. It was a crude sort of entertainment too; its lighter pieces were a mixture of coarse farce and naïve, fairy-tale plot, relieved by singing and dancing; while its more serious efforts were incoherent melodramas made lively by as many ghosts and massacres and maniacs as could be packed into them. Such a drama did not rise to the level of literature at all. Indeed it might never have done so, had it not been that a poor bohemian scholar, Marlowe (1564–1593), turned to the theatre as a means of making a living. Considered purely as a play-wright, Marlowe was not much improvement on his predecessors. He had no sense of character and no gift of construction. But he was a dramatic poet of genius: and, in his hands, these rough melodramas were transfigured into a vehicle for the soul-stirring expression of human passion.

> Ah Faustus,
> Now hast thou but one bare hower to liue,
> And then thou must be damnd perpetually:

19

Stand stil you euer moouing spheres of heauen,
That time may cease, and midnight neuer come:
Faire Natures eie, rise, rise againe, and make
Perpetuall day, or let this houre be but
A yeere, a moneth, a weeke, a naturall day,
That Faustus may repent, and saue his soule,
O lente, lente curite noctis equi:
The starres mooue stil, time runs, the clocke wil
   strike,
The diuel wil come, and Faustus must be damnd.

From the last soliloquy of DOCTOR FAUSTUS

In line after line of triumphant eloquence, Marlowe trumpets forth his Elizabethan pride in man's strength and beauty, his insatiable thirst for every joy, sensual and intellectual, that life could offer.

He was followed by a writer who, to a poetic genius even richer than his own, added that talent for design and character-drawing that he lacked. The peculiar significance of Shakespeare (1564–1616) in the history of English literature arises from the fact that it was he alone who had the capacity to impose order on the brilliant chaos of Elizabethan drama. He was not a revolutionary. His comedies and tragedies are compounded of the same elements as those of his contemporaries. They are the same extraordinary mixture of beauty and farce and improbable horrors. But the apparent defects of the form become in his hands virtues. The breadth and flexibility of his imagination enabled him to unite these elements into a whole, and to make use of their diversity to present a wider range of experience than could have been included in any stricter form.

> To die, to sleep;
> To sleep: perchance to dream: ay, there's the rub;
> For in that sleep of death what dreams may come
> When we have shuffled off this mortal coil,
> Must give us pause: there's the respect
> That makes calamity of so long life;
> For who would bear the whips and scorns of time,
> The oppressor's wrong, the proud man's contumely,
> The pangs of despised love, the law's delay,
> The insolence of office and the spurns
> That patient merit of the unworthy takes,
> When he himself might his quietus make,
> With a bare bodkin? who would fardels bear,
> To grunt and sweat under a weary life,
> But that the dread of something after death,
> The undiscover'd country from whose bourn
> No traveller returns, puzzles the will
> And makes us rather bear those ills we have
> Than fly to others that we know not of?
>
> *From HAMLET*

In his most characteristic plays, *Hamlet* and *Antony and Cleopatra*, he shows us life in its variety; he ranges from tragic passion to ironical comedy, from solid realistic portraiture to ethereal lyric beauty. Yet all is fused into a whole, by the life-giving form of his imagination. It does not matter if his stories are improbable: the people in them are so living that we believe anything that we are told of them. It does not matter that his plays are such a mixture: we only feel them truer to the heterogeneous nature of life. He has his limitations. Absorbed as he was in the huge spectacle of human existence moving before his gaze, his eye never wanders to explore the realms of spiritual light and darkness extending beyond the brief span of mortal experience.

> We are such stuff
> As dreams are made of. And our little life
> Is rounded with a sleep.

So runs the brief, baffled comment in which, in his last play, he seems to sum up his final conclusions on the riddle of human destiny. He is the supreme spectator; content to report what he sees, and to let us draw a lesson from it, if we can.

His specifically poetic quality is of a piece with the rest of his work. Shakespeare's is a dramatic style, designed to convey as realistically as possible, the flux of thought and feeling passing through the minds of his characters. To achieve this object he uses every means; breaks the ordinary rules of grammar and syntax, coins words of his own and employs any sort of language,

Scene from *The Taming of the Shrew* –
an engraving from the first illustrated edition
of Shakespeare, edited by Nicholas Rowe, 1709.

from slang to the most ornate poetic diction, without regard to conventional canons of style. He can write with classic restraint; but his genius is of the English and Gothic type, bold and fantastic, its simplest statement thickly embroidered with the images of his exuberant fancy. On occasion, his invention over-reaches itself. In his efforts to extend the frontiers of expression, he becomes obscure or bombastic; sometimes, too, his delight in his command over words leads him into playing tricks with them, inexcusable by any standard of good taste. But when all is said he has the most wonderful style in the world, able to convey at once a subtler and wider range of feeling than any other and in which word and thought are so closely identified that it is impossible to paraphrase his lines without losing their essential significance; while to crown all, he writes with a natural imperial magic that makes the work of other writers seem pale or laboured by comparison.

SONNET

When, in disgrace with Fortune and men's eyes,
I all alone beweep my outcast state,
And trouble deaf heaven with my bootless cries,
And look upon myself and curse my fate,
Wishing me like to one more rich in hope,
Featured like him, like him with friends possest,
Desiring this man's art and that man's scope,
With that I most enjoy contented least;

Yet in these thoughts myself almost despising –
Haply I think on thee: and then my state,
Like to the Lark at break of day arising,
From sullen earth, sings hymns at Heaven's gate;
For thy sweet love rememb'red such wealth brings
That then I scorn to change my state with kings.

Shakespeare's early work is gorgeous and sunshiny;
in maturity it is complex, sombre, weighed down with
the burden of thought. Here his work is a bridge
between the first Renaissance period and the second.
For the golden confidence of Spenser and Marlowe did
not last long. How should it? 'The glories of our blood
and state, are shadows, not substantial things.' And
those who pursue them most recklessly, are the soonest
to discover their vanity. The poets of the later Renais-
sance retained the vitality of the earlier: life to them
remained equally fascinating. But they did not trust it in
the same way. With anguish they recognised that its
pleasures and achievements are transitory; they are
incessantly aware of the inevitability of death, the mys-
terious uncertainty of fate, the appalling possibilities of
sin and suffering inherent in the very nature of human
existence. The dramas of the great play-wrights who
followed Shakespeare: Webster, Tourneur, Ford, are
glittering nightmares in which figures of baleful splen-
dour, burn their lives out against a lurid background of
blood and mania and supernatural darkness. Even the

John Donne (1572–1631).

one great comedian of the period, Ben Jonson (1573–1637), is touched with the same spirit. With fierce laughter, he ruthlessly exposes the monstrous pageant of human vice and folly.

Non-dramatic poetry shows the same change of heart. It is dominated by one man, John Donne (1573–1631). Donne is the epitome of the new age. In youth a passionate amorist, in age a passionate mystic, he thirsted as unappeasably as Marlowe himself for the absolute and the perfect. But a darker temperament, reinforced by the questionings of a restless powerful intelligence taught him that such perfection is never achieved in this world. Now and again he reaches his ideal; passion and intellect fuse together to attain a white heat of sensual or spiritual ecstasy unique in English poetry. More often, however, they struggle with one another in labyrinths of baffled thought. His mode of expression faithfully mirrors his divided spirit. Gone is the smooth sweetness of Spenser and his friends. Donne's language is colloquial, his rhythms complex, his imagery audacious and grotesque. For pages together he speaks in harsh and puzzling riddles; then suddenly comes a passage whose every word quivers, shining and transparent as a living flame.

Dear Love, for nothing less than thee
Would I have broke this happy dream,
   It was a theme

For reason, much too strong for fantasy.
Therefore thou waked'st me wisely; yet
My dream thou brok'st not, but continued'st it.
Thou art so true that thoughts of thee suffice
To make dreams truths and fables histories;
Enter these arms, for since thou thought'st it best
Not to dream all my dream, let's act the rest.

As lightning, or a taper's light,
Thine eyes, and not thy noise, waked me;
    Yet I thought thee –
For thou lov'st truth – an angel, at first sight;
But when I saw thou saw'st my heart,
And knew'st my thoughts beyond an angel's art
When thou knew'st what I dreamt, when thou knew'st
    when
Excess of joy would wake me, and cam'st then,
I must confess it could not choose but be
Profane to think thee anything but thee.

From THE DREAM

'Donne,' said Ben Jonson, 'was the first poet in the world in some things.' Certainly his contemporaries thought so. His influence was overwhelming. He had made lyrical poetry modern, individual and intellectual: after him it was almost impossible to go on writing in the conventional mode of the previous age. A host of writers appeared, ranging from pious clergymen to flaunting cavaliers, who sought to emulate Donne's boldness of style and fantastic ingenuities of thought. None of them was of his calibre of genius. But he had managed to communicate to them something of his intensity. So that they all have occasional flashes equal to the work of the greatest poets. Among the religious poets is the tender Herbert, the mystical Vaughan, the fiery Crashaw. The most famous of the secular are King, Carew, Suckling and the gallant Lovelace. Andrew Marvell (1621–1678) is the least unequal of Donne's followers.

Had we but World enough, and Time,
This coyness Lady were no crime.
We would sit down, and think which way
To walk, and pass our long Loves Day.

But at my back I alwaies hear
Times winged Charriot hurrying near:
And yonder all before us lye
Deserts of vast eternity.
Thy Beauty shall no more be found;
Nor, in thy marble Vault, shall sound
My echoing Song: then Worms shall try
That long preserv'd Virginity:
And your quaint Honour turn to dust;
And into ashes all my Lust.

From TO HIS COY MISTRESS

Robert Herrick (1591–1674).

Only two important writers withstood Donne's spell, Herrick and Milton. Herrick (1591–1674) is the least solemn of English poets. His pagan spirit was cheerfully impervious to melancholy thought. Gaily he continued to sing of springtime revels and light love, of curds and cream and nosegays. But he enjoyed them so freshly, he wrote with such a fanciful felicity that, touched by his hand, these withered flowers of poetry bloom anew, with a dewy and immortal sweetness.

UPON JULIA'S CLOTHES

Whenas in silks my Julia goes,
Then, then (me thinks) how sweetly flowes
That liquefaction of her clothes.

Next, when I cast mine eyes and see
That brave Vibration each way free;
Oh how that glittering taketh me!

There is nothing trifling about Milton (1608–1674). A scholar, a philosopher and a puritan, he thought all except the most elevated type of poetry not worth the writing, and from an early age he made it his object to be the great English master of such poetry, to enshrine in imperishable words the highest truths known to man. Such an ambition revealed an awe-inspiring confidence in his own powers. But it was justified. Milton's genius united, in a unique way, heroic loftiness of spirit with

31

the most delicate sensibility to every kind of sensuous beauty. He was also, alike in design and detail a master of his craft. His early work is jewelled and fanciful; the great religious poems of his later years are sublime and austere. But each is equally remarkable for the grandeur with which it is conceived and the lucid perfection with which it is executed.

DESCRIPTION OF SATAN AND THE FALLEN ANGELS

He above the rest
In shape and gesture proudly eminent
Stood like a Towr; his form had yet not lost
All her Original brightness, nor appear'd
Less than Arch Angel ruind, and th' excess
Of Glory obscur'd: As when the Sun new ris'n
Looks through the Horizontal misty Air
Shorn of his Beams, or from behind the Moon
In dim Eclipse disastrous twilight sheds
On half the Nations, and with fear of change
Perplexes Monarchs. Dark'n'd so, yet shon
Above them all th' Arch Angel: but his face
Deep scars of Thunder had intrencht, and care
Sat on his faded cheek, but under Browes
Of dauntless courage, and considerate Pride
Waiting revenge.

From PARADISE LOST

William Shakespeare (1564–1616).

Andrew Marvell (1621-1678).

Milton is the great example in English literature of that un-English type, the conscious artist; whose every effect is carried out in accordance with the rules of a refined and disciplined taste. His style is all marble and precious stones; it lacks Shakespeare's flexibility and still more his natural magic; but it is incapable of Shakespeare's lapses.

AT A SOLEMN MUSICK

Blest pair of Sirens, pledges of Heav'ns joy,
Sphear-born harmonious Sisters, Voice, and Vers,
Wed your divine sounds, and mixt power employ
Dead things with inbreath'd sense able to pierce,
And to our high-rais'd phantasie present,
That undisturbed Song of pure content,
Ay sung before the saphire-coloured throne
To him that sits thereon
With saintly shout, and solemn Jubily,
Where the bright Seraphim in burning row
Their loud up-lifted Angel trumpets blow,
And the Cherubick host in thousand quires,
Touch their immortal Harps of golden wires,
With those just Spirits that wear victorious Palms,
Hymns devout and holy Psalms
Singing everlastingly;
That we on Earth with undiscording voice
May rightly answer that melodious noise;
As once we did, till disproportion'd sin
Jarr'd against natures chime, and with harsh din

Broke the fair musick that all creatures made
To their great Lord, whose love their motion sway'd
In perfect Diapason, whilst they stood
In first obedience, and their state of good.
O may we soon again renew that Song,
And keep in tune with Heav'n till God ere long
To his celestial consort us unite,
To live with him, and sing in endless morn of light.

III

MILTON MARKS THE END OF THE GREAT AGE. HIS LIFE coincided with those civil and religious wars, in which the English Renaissance sank to extinction. The period which succeeded it was without the sensual and spiritual splendour of its predecessor; it lacked, also, its confusion and its extravagance. England in the late seventeenth and eighteenth centuries was a society settled in civilised equilibrium, untroubled by fundamental issues, and in which questions of conduct and manners were discussed by the standards of good sense and good taste. Such a society expressed itself in a very different sort of poetry from what had gone before; so different that subsequent generations, dazzled by the glories of the age of Shakespeare, have often denied that it was poetry at all. This shows, however, a foolishly narrow conception of poetry. The poets of this third phase may not be of the highest kind; but they have expressed perfectly certain aspects of human experience, not treated by other English poets. Theirs is

John Milton (1608-1674).

predominantly social poetry. It deals not with the ele-
mental passions of man, nor with his solitary dreams
and visions, but with those subjects that interest him as
a member of an organised society with established
standards and conventions. It is the poetry of home and
town and fashionable life, of friendship, flirtation and
worldly wisdom: it voices the normal person's affections
and his reflections on the way of the world. Its most
characteristic forms are satire, didactic verse and poems
of graceful compliment. When it fails it is commonplace
and conventional; it is successful by reason of its wit,
elegance and rhetorical force.

Dryden (1631–1700), who introduced the new style
of poetry, is the least personal of English poets. He was
a great critic; and even in his creative work he seems
stimulated to write less by desire to communicate an
individual vision, than by his pleasure in practising the
craft of letters. In consequence he is at his best in satire,
where his wit and vigour of mind compensates for any
lack of more imaginative qualities. But he tried his hand
at many other forms, songs, plays, stories; and always
with a fair degree of success. His most commonplace
thoughts are warmed into poetry by the sheer virile
accomplishment of his writing, the swing and snap of
his superb versification.

John Dryden (1631-1700).

ZIMRI

Some of their chiefs were princes of the land;
In the first rank of these did Zimri stand,
A man so various that he seemed to be
Not one, but all mankind's epitome;
Stiff in opinions, always in the wrong,
Was everything by starts and nothing long;
But in the course of one revolving moon
Was chymist, fiddler, statesman, and buffoon;
Then all for women, painting, rhyming, drinking,
Besides ten thousand freaks that died in thinking.
Blest madman, who could every hour employ,
With something new to wish or to enjoy!
Railing and praising were his usual themes,
And both, to show his judgment, in extremes:
So over violent or over civil
That every man with him was God or Devil.
In squandering wealth was his peculiar art;
Nothing went unrewarded but desert.
Beggared by fools whom still he found too late,
He had his jest, and they had his estate.

His most famous successor, Pope (1688–1744), is also
a master of his craft; not so varied but with an extremely
delicate sense of style which he polished to the last
degree of gleaming finish. Like that of the spider in one
of his own poems, Pope's touch: 'So exquisitely fine,
feels in each thread and lives along the line.' As Dryden
represents the strength of the new school, so Pope

Alexander Pope (1688-1744).

represents its elegance, its acute perception of detail in character and custom, and all intensified by the fire of his peculiar and waspish temperament. In his satires hate becomes positively beautiful, a glittering rapier piercing the heart of its victim with one graceful deadly thrust; his lighter poems, notably the *Rape of the Lock*, a fantasy about fashionable life, are the very triumph of artifice. The frills and airy frivolity of the beau monde are crystallised into sparkling immortality by the brilliance of his art.

THE LADY'S DRESSING TABLE

And now, unveil'd, the Toilet stands display'd,
Each silver Vase in mystic order laid.
This casket India's glowing gems unlocks,
And all Arabia breathes from yonder box.
The Tortoise here and Elephant unite,
Transform'd to combs, the speckled, and the white.
Here files of pins extend their shining rows,
Puffs, Powders, Patches, Bibles, Billet-doux.
Now awful Beauty puts on all its arms;
The fair each moment rises in her charms,
Repairs her smiles, awakens every grace,
And calls forth all the wonders of her face.

From THE RAPE OF THE LOCK

Pope set the standard of taste for his age. Indeed for sixty years after his death, writers, some of them very gifted, like Goldsmith and Doctor Johnson, took him as their model. He had, however, reached perfection in his kind; and none of his followers equalled him. Fortunately, some poets did not try. The eighteenth century saw the rise of a number of authors – Thomson and Gray, Collins and Cowper, are the most famous of them – who turned from the urban and social subjects which had engaged the pens of Pope and Dryden, to sing in quieter strains of the pleasures of retirement. They represent no violent break with the prevailing tradition. As much as Dryden and Pope, they were rational and civilised persons, accepting the standards of society in which they lived: as much as Dryden and Pope they spoke for the average intelligent man of their day. Only they spoke for him in his more contemplative and sentimental moods. They express his love for friends and home, his sober piety, his pleasure in the peaceful beauty of the countryside. As life becomes more urban, people grow more consciously appreciative of nature as such. Spenser and Milton do not draw any careful distinction between natural beauty and other beauty; they enjoy both because they are beautiful. To Thomson (1700–1748) and Cowper (1731–1800), the untutored charm of the rural and the rustic makes a peculiar appeal; living in a sophisticated world, the unsophisticated has for them the attraction of contrast, and their eighteenth-century eye for reality makes them describe it with delightful accuracy. The English

William Cowper (1731-1800).

landscape appears in their pages just as it is, undisguised by the extravagance of poetic fancy. Thomson, with his grassy distances stretching beneath sun-lit or cloudy skies, paints the broader view of it: Cowper's is more delicately exact in detail. He is memorable too as the only distinguished poet who has found his chief inspiration in domesticity, in the Englishman's characteristic tenderness for the simple pleasures and steadfast affections of home life, his sentiment for his own house, his own garden, his own pet animals.

EPITAPH ON A TAME HARE

Here lies, whom hound did ne'er pursue,
    Nor swifter greyhound follow,
Whose foot ne'er tainted morning dew,
    Nor ear heard huntsman's halloo;

* * *

Old Tiney, surliest of his kind,
    Who, nursed with tender care,
And to domestic hounds confined,
    Was still a wild Jack hare.

* * *

His diet was of wheaten bread,
    And milk, and oats, and straw;
Thistles, or lettuces instead,
    With sand to scour his maw.

* * *

But now beneath this walnut shade
   He finds his long last home,
And waits, in snug concealment laid,
   Till gentler Puss shall come.

Gray (1716–1771) and Collins (1721–1759) are less fertile writers. Their combined works only make up a slender volume of elegiac verses, in most of which pensive reflection is diversified by occasional vignettes of landscape. In Collins' poems these vignettes play the largest part; he was the more imaginative of the two. Gray had a greater mastery of design, strengthened by a deeper note of sentiment.

In neither do we find the warmth of temperament necessary to raise them to the highest levels of poetry. But both have achieved a permanent place in English letters, by the purity of their inspiration, and the scholarly grace with which they have clothed it.

Some village-Hampden, that with dauntless breast
   The little Tyrant of his fields withstood,
Some mute inglorious Milton here may rest,
   Some Cromwell guiltless of his country's blood.

Th' applause of list'ning senates to command,
   The threats of pain and ruin to despise,
To scatter plenty o'er a smiling land,
   And read their hist'ry in a nation's eyes,

Their lot forbad: nor circumscrib'd alone
   Their growing virtues, but their crimes confin'd;
Forbad to wade through slaughter to a throne,
   And shut the gates of mercy on mankind,

* * *

Far from the madding crowd's ignoble strife,
   Their sober wishes never learn'd to stray;
Along the cool sequester'd vale of life
   They kept the noiseless tenor of their way.

From Gray's ELEGY IN A COUNTRY CHURCH-
   YARD

How sleep the brave, who sink to rest,
By all their countries wishes blest!
When Spring, with dewy fingers cold,
Returns to deck their hallow'd mould,
She there shall dress a sweeter sod,
Than Fancy's feet have ever trod.

By fairy hands their knell is rung,
By forms unseen their dirge is sung;
Their Honour comes, a pilgrim gray,
To bless the turf that wraps their clay,
And Freedom shall awhile repair,
To dwell a weeping hermit there!

William Collins

Both the urban and the country schools have left
their mark on the work of the last important writer in
the eighteenth-century tradition. George Crabbe

46

Thomas Gray (1716-1771)

(1754–1832) was not a polished artist. The long bleak narratives of rural life, which make up the greater part of his work are often written in a style as bare as a guide-book; but there is something compelling about them. The patient accuracy with which he observes the world, the unillusioned wisdom with which he judges it, make one listen to his words and forbid one to forget them.

From the general tradition of this period of English verse, two names stand apart. Robert Burns (1759–1796), a Scottish peasant, founded his work on the popular songs of his own Lowland countryside, and it has the direct infectious zest and songfulness of a ballad. But heaven had made him a great artist; he added to the natural qualities of folk-poetry, a grace, a finish and a humour of his own. The elemental feelings of humanity, the massive fun and pathos and passion of the natural man become, in his hands, the stuff of immortal poetry:

> Ye flowery bank o' bonnie Doon,
> How can ye blume sae fair!
> How can ye chant ye little birds,
> And I sae fu' o' care.

> Thou'll break my heart, thou bonnie bird,
> That sings upon the bough:
> Thou minds me of the happy days,
> When my fause luve was true.

William Blake (1757–1827) is a more unusual type. He is in every respect a sensational contrast to his contemporaries. Possibly insane, and certainly inspired, he passed most of his time in a realm of mystical visions from which the material world was hardly visible, but which was astir with mysterious figures of demon and angel. An experience so remote from that of ordinary people makes much of Blake's work strange, and even unintelligible. But he had a lyrical gift of such unearthly power as to render this of almost no consequence. His fleeting fragments of song, his wild prophetic rhapsodies contain the distilled essence of poetry. They set the reader's nerves athrill with the inexplicable force of some natural manifestation, the cry of the birds, or the rush of the wind in the tree-tops.

JERUSALEM

And did those feet in ancient time
    Walk upon England's mountains green?
And was the holy Lamb of God
    On England's pleasant pastures seen?

And did the Countenance Divine
    Shine forth upon our clouded hills?
And was Jerusalem builded here
    Among these dark Satanic Mills?

Bring me my bow of burning gold!
    Bring me my arrows of desire!
Bring me my spear! O clouds, unfold!
    Bring me my chariot of fire!

I will not cease from mental fight,
    Nor shall my sword sleep in my hand,
Till we have built Jerusalem
    In England's green and pleasant land.

William Blake (1757-1827).

IV

BLAKE LIVED BEFORE HIS TIME. HIS OWN AGE COULD NOT be expected to appreciate him; but in the forty years that followed his death, once more a revolution took place in English letters. Under the double shock of the Industrial and French revolutions, the fabric of eighteenth-century civilisation crumbled; its standards of taste and conduct lost their hold, and people turned for guidance to the instinctive movements of the heart and imagination. In politics and practical life this led to a good deal of confusion. Poetry however profited by the change. For passion and imagination are essential ingredients of the best poetry. Now, after a hundred years repression, they flared up in the brightest blaze of poetic splendour since the Renaissance. It was marked by many of the same qualities. Glamour and mystery, extravagance and irregularity, fantasy and naïvety came thronging back into literature. But the poets of this new Romantic school, as it was called, were more consciously individualistic than the Elizabethans; reacting violently against the conventions that had governed their fathers, they deliberately followed the light of their vision wherever it might lead them. And they concentrated more on the inner life. They turned from the humdrum world to seek inspiration in the secret dreams of the fancy and the adventures of the solitary soul.

Wordsworth (1770–1850), the first great poet of the period, was a mystic of nature. The mountains of that Lake country of north-west England which was his home, its still waters and wooded silences communicated to him the sense of an indwelling spirit of the Universe, divine and beneficent, who would, if man listened to its voice, illuminate him with its own ineffable wisdom. To interpret this voice to mankind was the aim of all Wordsworth's poetry; and he thought this was best done by expressing himself in the plainest language, undisguised by the artificial ornaments of conscious art. Only a writer with the most impeccable natural taste could follow this principle without danger. Wordsworth was far from being such an author. The result is that his work is ludicrously unequal. Often it is as flat as the flattest prose. But now and then inspiration seizes him: and he rises to a height of serene, spiritual sublimity unparalleled in English poetry. Moreover, unlike Blake, he is never so rapt into the world of his vision as to lose sight of the common earth. He is the supreme poet of spiritual experience, who can both convey those moments of celestial glory, in which man

William Wordsworth (1770-1850).

penetrates beyond the veil of the flesh, and also show
them in their true relation to the confined prosaic round
of every day existence.

> But now, like one who rows,
> Proud of his skill, to reach a chosen point
> With an unswerving line, I fixed my view
> Upon the summit of a craggy ridge,
> The horizon's utmost boundary; far above
> Was nothing but the stars and the grey sky.
> She was an elfin pinnace; lustily
> I dipped my oars into the silent lake,
> And, as I rose upon the stroke, my boat
> Went heaving through the water like a swan;
> When, from behind that craggy steep till then
> The horizon's bound, a huge peak, black and huge,
> As if with voluntary power instinct
> Upreared its head. I struck and struck again,
> And growing still in stature the grim shape
> Towered up between me and the stars, and still,
> For so it seemed, with purpose of its own
> And measured motion like a living thing,
> Strode after me. With trembling oars I turned,
> And through the silent water stole my way
> Back to the covert of the willow tree;
> There in her mooring-place I left my bark,–
> And through the meadows homeward went, in grave
> And serious mood; but after I had seen
> That spectacle, for many days, my brain
> Worked with a dim and undertermined sense

Of unknown modes of being; o'er my thoughts
There hung a darkness, call it solitude
Or blank desertion. No familiar shapes
Remained, no pleasant images of trees,
Of sea or sky, no colours of green fields;
But huge and mighty forms, that do not live
Like living men, moved slowly through the mind
By day, and were a trouble to my dreams.

From THE PRELUDE

Wordsworth's friend, Coleridge (1772–1834), had no such definite gospel to expound. He was a man of the most varied gifts, critic and philosopher as well as poet. And in each capacity, he exhibited gleams of extraordinary genius. But, owing to some inexplicable inability to concentrate his powers, they only found complete fulfilment in a handful of poems. The most famous of these, *The Ancient Mariner*, and *Christabel*, reveal another aspect of the romantic impulse, its sensibility to the imaginative appeal of the remote and the marvellous. In a succession of pictures, preternaturally vivid as those of a dream, and set to a haunting word music, they evoke the eerie enchantment of medieval legend.

The moving Moon went up the sky,
And nowhere did abide;
Softly she was going up,
And a star or two beside–
Her beams bemock'd the sultry main,
Like April hoar-frost spread;
But where the ship's huge shadow lay,
A still and awful red.

Beyond the shadow of the ship,
I watched the water-snakes:
They moved in tracks of shining white,
And when they rear'd, the elfish light
Fell off in hoary flakes.

Within the shadow of the ship,
I watch'd their rich attire:
Blue, glossy green, and velvet black,
They coil'd and swam, and every track
Was a flash of golden fire.

From THE ANCIENT MARINER

A similar sensibility, but this time to the picturesque
appeal of true history, is the outstanding characteristic
of Sir Walter Scott's poems. Scott (1771–1832) was
primarily a novelist; his rousing ballad tales in verse are
poetry for boys rather than men. As such, however, they
are as good as possible, stirring and gallant as the sight
of a regiment stepping out to the sound of drum and
bugle. The other romantic poets, Keats, Shelley, Byron,

Samuel Taylor Coleridge (1772-1834).

rise higher. Keats (1795–1821) like Coleridge responded to the attraction of medieval literature. But in him this was only one expression of a feeling for beauty of every kind. 'I have loved the principal of beauty in all things,' he said, and the object of his poetry was to express this love. He was equipped to do it. Not only could he appreciate beauty in its most varied manifestations, but he had an extraordinary faculty for detecting precisely the qualities, in which each specific manifestation consisted. Keats died very young, at the age of twenty-five, before he had learnt to discipline his exuberant talent; and some of his work is marred by a youthful floridity. But he had a gift for the right word, for the exact visualising phrase that can only be compared to Shakespeare's.

ON FIRST LOOKING INTO CHAPMAN'S HOMER

Much have I travell'd in the realms of gold,
    And many goodly states and kingdoms seen;
    Round many western islands have I been
Which bards in fealty to Apollo hold.
Oft of one wide expanse had I been told
    That deep-brow'd Homer ruled as his demesne;
    Yet did I never breathe its pure serene
Till I heard Chapman speak out loud and bold:
Then felt I like some watcher of the skies
    When a new planet swims into his ken;
Or like stout Cortez when with eagle eyes

PERCY B. SHELLEY.

Percy Bysshe Shelley (1792-1822).

He stared at the Pacific – and all his men
Look'd at each other with a wild surmise–
    Silent, upon a peak in Darien.

In his pages, spring and autumn, the sensuous grace of classic myth, the moon-lit forests of fairy-tale, rise before the mental eye in all the detailed, breathing loveliness of reality.

Shelley (1792–1822) is the lyrical poet of the movement. Take it all in all, he is the most wonderful lyrical poet England has ever produced. In flight after flight of soaring, full-throated song he gives voice to those aspirations after an ideal freedom alike in love and politics, which surge in the breasts of the youth of his time. Youthfulness is one of Shelley's outstanding qualities. He has all youth's enthusiasm, its dreamy exaltation, its refusal to compromise with evil. Indeed, his idealism often made him very unhappy. His mood hovered between rapture at life as he wished it to be and despair at life as he found it. This division of spirit was, however, to the advantage of his poetry. For it kept it from becoming inhuman. His songs glow with an ethereal radiance, but they also throb with the poignancy of a soul who has known what it is to suffer.

Asia. The rocks are cloven, and through the purple night
    I see cars drawn by rainbow-winged steeds
    Which trample the dim winds: in each there stands
    A wild-eyed charioteer urging their flight.

61

Some look behind, as fiends pursued them there,
And yet I see no shapes but the keen stars:
Others, with burning eyes, lean forth, and drink
With eager lips the wind of their own speed,
As if the thing they loved fled on before,
And now, even now, they clasped it.
Their bright locks
Stream like a comet's flashing hair: they all
Sweep onward.

Demogorgon. These are the immortal Hours,
Of whom thou didst demand. One waits for thee.

From PROMETHEUS UNBOUND

There is nothing of Shelley's innocence about Byron (1788–1824). A dynamic, theatrical personality, ruthlessly observant of other people and morbidly sensitive to their opinion of himself he both lived and wrote with one eye fixed upon his audience. They returned his gaze. The figure of the beautiful Lord Byron with his reckless brilliance, and his shocking thrilling career of love and lawlessness, caught the imagination of the public as no poet ever has before or since. Since then a reaction has set in. Byron, in his own day far more admired than Keats or Shelley, is now rated below them. This is partly just; there is something coarse and stagey about his talent. But the decline of his reputation is also due to a passing fashion in taste. During the nineteenth century the standard of poetry was set by the other romantics; writers were admired in so far as they exhibited their sort of merit. Although Byron's life was romantic, his literary gifts were nearer those of Dryden and Pope. Like them he was a brilliant and eloquent commentator on the active life of man. And he was their equal. His best works, *Don Juan* and *The Vision of Judgment*, are written with a careless scintillating mastery that keep them as vital now, as the day they were written.

ON HIMSELF

My days of love are over; me no more
    The charms of maid, wife, and still less of widow,
Can make the fool of which they made before,–
    In short, I must not lead the life I did do;
The credulous hope of mutual minds is o'er,
    The copious use of claret is forbid too,
So for a good old-gentlemanly vice,
I think I must take up with avarice.

Ambition was my idol, which was broken
    Before the shrines of Sorrow, and of Pleasure;
And the two last have left me many a token,
    O'er which reflection may be made at leisure:
Now, like Friar Bacon's brazen head, I've spoken,
    'Time is, Time was, Time's past;' – a chymic
      treasure
Is glittering youth, which I have spent betimes –
My heart in passion, and my head on rhymes.

From DON JUAN

One other poet of this period must not be forgotten. Walter Savage Landor (1775–1864) is one of those authors who seem to have been created by Providence to show that there is an exception to every rule. He is equally far from the school of Pope and the school of the Romantics. The chief influence we can trace in his work is that of the ancient Latin writers. The epigrams which are his chief claim to fame, so grand in conception and so tersely expressed, are like antique inscriptions carved in marble to last for ever.

SEPARATION

There is a mountain and a wood between us,
  Where the lone shepherd and late bird have seen
  us
Morning and noon and eventide repass.
Between us now the mountain and the wood
Seem standing darker than last year they stood,
  And say we must not cross – alas! alas!

Meanwhile the tide of romanticism swept irresistibly on. Its first dazzling outburst came to an end with Byron. But the movement did not spend itself for a century and more; and produced a succession of poets who, if they never rose as high as their masters, maintained nevertheless a very high level. The first phase

John Keats (1795–1821).

Lord Byron (1788–1824).

was distinguished by three figures, Tennyson, Browning and Matthew Arnold. Tennyson (1809–1892) was, poetically speaking, the child of Keats; stimulated to write by a similar sensibility to beauty and with a natural gift for the lovely evocative phrase. He was a more accomplished craftsman, and his best work is a miracle of finished art. Only – he lacked Keats's divine fire. Perfectly though he expresses it, his vision of beauty has not the same inspired intensity; after Keats the best of Tennyson seems a little undistinguished. This lack of distinction was increased by the fact that he seldom allowed himself to concentrate exclusively on his vision. By the time he reached his maturity the Victorian age had begun to dawn over England. The Victorian age, strenuous and puritanical, took the view that poetry should teach a moral lesson. Tennyson yielded to the pressure of his age: he set up to be preacher as well as poet. And since his preaching did not spring from his native creative impulse, it was uninspired; a mere polished repetition of opinions held by serious persons of his day. All the same Tennyson is a great poet. No one since has left a volume of verse covering so wide a range of subject, with such consistent mastery of the art of writing. Moreover he has a special interest as one of the best painters of the English scene. Eastern and southern England are portrayed in his verses with the detailed accuracy of Cowper and a silvery exquisiteness of phrase, all his own.

Alfred Lord Tennyson (1809–1892).

Now fades the last long streak of snow,
   Now burgeons every maze of quick
   About the flowering square, and thick
By ashen roots the violets blow.

Now rings the woodland loud and long,
   The distance takes a lovelier hue,
   And drown'd in yonder living blue
The lark becomes a sightless song.

Now dance the lights on lawn and lea,
   The flocks are whiter down the vale,
   And milkier every milky sail
On winding stream or distant sea.

From IN MEMORIAM

No one ever accused Browning (1812–1889) of yielding to convention. In him, we find the wilful determination of the romantic to be himself at all costs, carried to its limit. The sort of poem he wrote – it was usually some spasmodic lyric or a dramatic monologue, put into the mouth of some curious imaginary character – is his own invention; so is his philosophy, a defiant optimism, boisterously welcoming disaster as a test of its strength. Most individual of all is his actual style; conversational, slap-dash, and freaked all over with the grotesque quips of Browning's fancy. So aggressively eccentric an author will never please every one. And it must be admitted Browning is often obscure and ugly. But he is most exciting reading: bursting with life and passion and possessed of a subtle insight into the processes of men's minds. He is also a most important influence, for what is looked on as the very 'modern' type of poetry, the complex, realistic, intellectual poetry of Mr. T. S. Eliot and his followers, derives directly from Browning.

LOVE IN A LIFE

Room after room,
I hunt the house through
We inhabit together.
Heart, fear nothing, for, heart, thou shalt find her,
Next time, herself! – not the trouble behind her
Left in the curtain, the couch's perfume!
As she brush'd it, the cornice-wreath blossom'd
    anew:
Yon looking-glass gleam'd at the wave of her feather.

Yet the day wears,
And door succeeds door;
I try the fresh fortune –
Range the wide house from the wing to the centre.
Still the same chance! she goes out as I enter.
Spend my whole day in the quest, – who cares?
But 'tis twilight you see, – with such suites to
    explore,
Such closets to search, such alcoves to importune!

Matthew Arnold (1822–1888) was a less original writer. He was a serious-minded academic person, learned in the literature of the past; his style is a careful blend of Wordsworth and the classics. In consequence it never stirs us with the first-hand creative freshness of Browning or Tennyson. But this deficiency is partly counterbalanced by a greater depth of sentiment. In words of restrained and poignant eloquence, Arnold voices the profound melancholy which was beginning to permeate the more thoughtful minds of his time. For, in spite of its outward prosperity, and the extraordinary advance of material improvement which it witnessed, the Victorian age was not serene. Intellectually it was disordered; the revolutionary movement, which pre-ceded it, had failed to establish any foundation of commonly accepted ideals, on which confidence in life might securely rest itself; religious faith was shaken by the discoveries of science. Darkly, the huge energy of material progress swept onwards to no certain end. This uncertainty affected the writers of the age and it was rendered still more painful for them by the fact that the new industrial civilisation, which was bit by bit super-seding the old England, tended to look on literature as a frivolous luxury, unrelated to the serious business of life. In consequence, the poets themselves grew more and more to feel at odds with the world in which they lived. Some turned their backs on it to take shelter in some secluded monastery of the imagination, constructed by themselves: others, embracing the philosophy of pessimism, openly repudiated life as a cheat. They can hardly be blamed. But it was a pity. It is not healthy for the artist to feel himself out of tune with the people round him. He becomes cranky or narrow or both. Whether for this cause or not, the poets of the later nineteenth century seem built on a smaller scale than their predecessors.

However they remained very good in quality. And there were a great many of them. The Pre-Raphaelite group, led by Rossetti (1828–1882) and William Morris (1834–1896) in his earliest most fruitful phase, found refuge in an artistic dreamland founded on the art and literature of the Middle Ages and early Renaissance. It was an artificial place. And their poetry is a little artificial: languid, over-decorated, and self-conscious. But it does achieve the beauty which is its object. Morris's clear-coloured medieval landscapes, with their belfried towns peopled by troops of heraldic figures, Rossetti's sultry Italian splendours; made melancholy by a brooding autumnal passion – these can still delight the eye of the imagination.

Edward FitzGerald (1809-1883).

NEAR AVALON

A ship with shield before the sun,
Six maidens round the mast,
A red-gold crown on every one,
A green gown on the last.

The fluttering green banners there
Are wrought with ladies' heads most fair,
And a portraiture of Guenevere
The middle of each sail doth bear..

A ship with sails before the wind,
And round the helm six knights,
Their heaumes are on, whereby, half blind,
They pass by many sights.

William Morris

Associated with these poets was Swinburne. Unlike
theirs, his was a lyrical talent, deriving from Shelley
rather than Keats: and though he too was deliberately
archaic in style, he was not so exclusively pre-
Raphaelite. His dream world included elements taken
from the Greeks and the Bible. Books rather than life
were his inspiration. Indeed he had so little of his own to
say, that his poetry is at times almost meaningless. But it
too had beauty; surging forth in a torrent of orchestral
music, all a-shimmer with sumptuous words.

Swinburne, in so far as he had a philosophy, was a
pessimist, tumultuously lamenting the vanity of all
things human. Here he links on to the declared pessi-

Dante Gabriel Rossetti (1828–1882).

mists. In Edward FitzGerald's *Rubaiyat of Omar Khayyám*, a very free adaptation from the Persian, pessimism was combined with a keen sensibility to pleasure. FitzGerald is a most original writer, mingling an eighteenth century wit and precision, with a dreamy Oriental exoticism of mood. Since all ends in dust, is the burden of his song, let us enjoy ourselves while we can. Nowhere else in English is this ancient philosophy expressed so memorably as in his chiming, tolling stanzas.

Ah, my Beloved, fill the Cup that clears
Today of past Regrets and future Fears –
   Tomorrow? – Why, Tomorrow I may be
Myself with Yesterday's Sev'n Thousand years.

Lo! some we loved, the loveliest and best
That Time and Fate of all their Vintage prest,
   Have drunk their Cup a Round or two before,
And one by one crept silently to Rest.

And we, that now make merry in the Room
They left, and Summer dresses in new Bloom,
   Ourselves must we beneath the Couch of Earth
Descend, ourselves to make a Couch – for whom?

Ah, make the most of what we yet may spend,
Before we too into the Dust descend;
   Dust into Dust, and under Dust, to lie,
Sans Wine, sans Song, sans Singer, and – sans End! . . .

From OMAR KHAYYAM

Equally beautiful, equally hopeless, are the lyrics of A. E. Housman, a Cambridge scholar, who came to maturity at the end of the century. Here the setting is not Oriental but rural. He called himself the Shropshire lad; and his pages are full of exquisite brief glimpses of the English landscape. But these only form an ironical background to a pessimism more intense than Fitz-Gerald's.

> Into my heart an air that kills
> From yon far country blows:
> What are those blue remembered hills,
> What spires, what farms are those?

> That is the land of lost content,
> I see it shining plain,
> The happy highways where I went
> And cannot come again.

Housman and FitzGerald are, for all their perfection, minor writers. Thomas Hardy is one of the great figures of English literature. We must read his novels to realise his full stature. His poems are often marred by a Browningesque roughness and quaintness. But, to a feeling for the countryside more intimate than Housman's, he joined an extraordinary nobility of spirit. Life to him was essentially tragic; a grim battle, in which man was almost certainly defeated by Fate. Yet he faces it

Thomas Hardy (1840-1928).

with a brave tender resignation, an unfailing compassion for helpless mortality, which somehow draws the sting from despair. Hardy's clumsy, plaintive strains have a mysterious power to soothe the heart, like the sight of the downland sky he loved so well.

THE END OF THE EPISODE

Indulge no more may we
In this sweet-bitter pastime:
The love-light shines the last time
    Between you, Sweet, and me.

There shall remain no trace
Of what so closely tied us,
And blank as ere love eyed us
    Will be our meeting-place.

The flowers and thymy air,
Will they now miss our coming?
The bumbles thin their humming
    To find we haunt not there?

Though fervent was our vow,
Though ruddily ran our pleasure,
Bliss has fulfilled its measure,
    And see its sentence now.

Ache deep; but make no moans:
Smile out; but still suffer
The paths of love are rougher
Than thoroughfares of stones.

Meanwhile, a few poets found security from the prevailing doubt, in the unchanging truths of religious faith. Coventry Patmore and Gerard Hopkins were Catholics. Both were original unequal writers, whose queer idiosyncrasies make them hard to appreciate at a first reading. Patmore was a follower of Donne, born two hundred years later, whose complex ingenious poetry strives to express a mystical vision mingling sensual and spiritual passion. Hopkins, a Jesuit priest, is difficult not for his thoughts but for his mode of expression. He was always experimenting in language and metre; at times so boldly as to be unintelligible. His successful experiments, however, have a vivid astonishing splendour.

The one great Anglican poet of the period is easy to admire. Rossetti's sister, Christina, expressed simple thoughts in simple language. But she was an inspired genius, in whom an exquisite sense of art was charged by a throbbing passion. Sometimes she sings of love, sometimes of religion; but always with pathetic loveliness. Her modest achievement is one of the most perfect in the whole of English literature.

Emily Brontë (1818–1848).

A BIRTHDAY

My heart is like a singing bird
    Whose nest is in a watered shoot;
My heart is like an apple-tree
    Whose boughs are bent with thickset fruit;
My heart is like a rainbow shell
    That paddles in a halcyon sea;
My heart is gladder than all these
    Because my love is come to me.

Christina Rossetti

Other poets with Christian beliefs are also memorable: Francis Thompson, sumptuous and impassioned, and the careful, sensitive Alice Meynell. Meanwhile a few other authors found confidence in life in creeds of their own. Emily Brontë, in a handful of verses, expressed a mysticism as fiery as Blake's; the coloured, complicated poetry of George Meredith proclaimed a belief in the ultimate benevolence of nature; Rudyard Kipling, famous also as a story-teller, made a religion of patriotism. His imaginative appreciation of England's romantic past, his triumphant belief in her imperial destiny, found expression in ringing strains that managed to make themselves heard far beyond the ordinary circle of readers of poetry, and sent their tunes lilting in the heads of Englishmen all over the world.

Finally two writers, living well into the twentieth century, brought Victorian poetry to a close in a fan-fare

Robert Browning (1812-1889).

William Morris (1834-1896).

of triumphant music. Their careers run curiously parallel. Robert Bridges, starting as a song writer in a smooth, traditional manner appeared in his last work the *Testament of Beauty*, as a philosophic poet, intellectual in subject matter and writing in an austere, highly experimental style; William Butler Yeats made his name as a sort of Irish Rossetti, the author of dreamy moon-lit poems set in a Celtic fairyland. In middle life he deliberately changed his style to become a poet of ideas, severe and rhetorical. Bridges and Yeats both founded their view of life on a belief in the absolute value of their art. They assert their conviction that beauty is its own justification. Here the likeness between them ends. Bridges has a thoroughly English talent combining a fastidious scholarly taste with a fresh bird-like sweetness. The beauty he worships is serene; its classic temple stands in the rich smiling quiet of English park-land.

> I love all beauteous things,
>   I seek and adore them;
> God hath no better praise,
> And man in his hasty days
>   Is honoured for them.
>
> I too will something make
>   And joy in the making;
> Altho' to-morrow it seem
> Like the empty words of a dream
>   Remembered on waking.

William Butler Yeats (1861-1939).

Very different is the gleaming shrine of Yeats's adoration, written with the cabalistic symbols of some secret mystery, and shadowed by the boughs of the Irish forest. For all the sophistication of his art, there is something untamed in Yeats's inspiration; for all his mastery of the English tongue, his genius is exotic.

I dreamed that one had died in a strange place
Near no accustomed hand;
And they had nailed the boards above her face
The peasants of that land,
And, wondering, planted by her solitude
A cypress and a yew:
I came, and wrote upon a cross of wood,
Man had no more to do:
She was more beautiful than thy first love,
This lady by the trees:
And gazed upon the mournful stars above,
And heard the mournful breeze.

V

L ONG BEFORE BRIDGES AND YEATS DIED, POETRY HAD entered on its modern phase. It is beyond the scope of this essay to try and estimate this. The writers of to-day have not been born into a happy age for poetry. The doubt and the despondency of the later nineteenth century, have been sharpened for them by the shock of world catastrophe. However, the poets have gone on writing; and though their work is fragmentary compared with that of their predecessors, it is full of originality and life. Individualistic and lyrical, it is still romantic in type. The Georgian poets, who flourished in the first twenty years of the century, were rural romantics. The most typical of them, Edward Thomas, Edmund Blunden and V. Sackville-West turned away from the unsympathetic atmosphere of industrial England to seek for peace in the homely charms of English country life. Contemporary with them, appeared the passionate, disordered rhapsodies of D. H. Lawrence, the sculptured eloquence of Hilaire Belloc, the fresh songs of W. H. Davies, the direct appeal of Masefield's poetry and above all the elfin loveliness of Walter de la Mare.

THE SCRIBE

What lovely things
   Thy hand hath made
The smooth-plumed bird
   In its emerald shade,
The seed of the grass
   The speck of stone
Which the wayfaring ant
   Stirs – and hastes on!

Though I should sit
   By some tarn in thy hills,
Using its ink
   As the spirit wills
To write of Earth's wonders,
   Its live, willed things,
Flit would the ages
   On soundless wings
Ere unto Z
   My pen drew nigh;
Leviathan told,
   And the honey-fly:

And still would remain
  My wit to try –
My worn reeds broken,
  The dark tarn dry,
All words forgotten –
  Thou, Lord, and I.

Walter de la Mare

These writers came to maturity before the war of 1914. They still retain something of the serenity of a former age. Even if they were dissatisfied with the world they knew, they felt confidence enough to build a world of their own. Those who felt the shock of the war when still quite young, found this impossible. During the war itself, England produced little poetry; only some poignant verses of hope by Rupert Brooke and others, at the beginning, and at the end some poignant verses of despair by Wilfred Owen and others; these were moving rather from their sincerity of feeling than their poetic excellence.

The bleak anti-climax of the peace brought forth a new school led by T. S. Eliot. These are romantics in full disillusionment, yearning vainly after ecstasy. Mr. Eliot is a Christian; his younger successors, Mr. Auden and Mr. Spender, seem to look for salvation to a kind of Communism; but both are so disheartened that neither the real world nor that of their dreams seems to give them any zest of inspiration. To express their frustrated

Rupert Brooke (1887–1915).

mood they have evolved a new style, complex, intellectual and ironical, modern in diction, broken in rhythm.

> What, at the time of the birth of Our Lord,
>   at Christmastide,
> Is there not peace upon earth, goodwill among men?
> The peace of this world is always uncertain, unless men
>   keep the peace of God.
> And war among men defiles this world, but death in the
>   Lord renews it,
> And the world must be cleaned in the winter, or we
>   shall have only
> A sour spring, a parched summer, an empty harvest.
> Between Christmas and Easter what work shall be done?
> The ploughman shall go out in March and turn the
>   same earth
> He has turned before, the bird shall sing the same
>   song.
> When the leaf is out on the trees, when the elder and
>   may
> Burst over the stream, and the air is clear and high,
> And voices trill at windows, and children tumble in
>   front of the door,
> What work shall have been done, what wrong
> Shall the bird's song cover, the green tree cover, what
>   wrong
> Shall the fresh earth cover? We wait, and the time is
>   short
> But waiting is long.

T. S. Eliot from MURDER IN THE CATHEDRAL

Such poetry is too obscure and too joyless ever to be widely popular. But at its best, it has a pungent fascination, softened by gleams of a wistful beauty. Dorothy Wellesley and W. J. Turner, in their imaginative and philosophical poetry, the Sitwells, Ruth Pitter in her religious verse, have not broken away from the main English tradition. They have contrived to set their modern thought to a music which is still rich with the overtones of past poetry.

Now once more war is sweeping the country. How far it will affect literature and in what direction, it is too early to say. But poetry seems by now so deeply rooted in the English nature, that it is impossible to believe it will ever be extinguished.

colour plates

Edmund Spenser (1552-1599)
Sir Walter Raleigh (1552-1618)
William Shakespeare (1564-1616)
Andrew Marvell (1621-1678)
John Keats (1795-1821)
Lord Byron (1788-1824)
Robert Browning (1812-1889)
William Morris (1834-1896)

black & white
illustrations

Percy Bysshe Shelley (1792-1822)
Alfred Lord Tennyson (1809-1892)
Edward FitzGerald (1809-1883)
Dante Gabriel Rossetti (1828-1882)
Thomas Hardy (1840-1928)
Emily Brontë (1818-1848)
William Butler Yeats (1861-1939)
Rupert Brooke (1887-1915)

Index

Acknowledgments

THE PUBLISHERS ARE GRATEFUL TO THE FOLLOWING for permission to publish extracts from copyright material – **Robert Bridges**: by kind permission of Lord Bridges and Oxford University Press. **Walter de la Mare**: The Society of Authors as the literary representative of the author's estate. **T. S. Eliot**: The Complete Poems and Plays, Faber and Faber Ltd., and (U.S.) Harcourt Brace and Company. **Thomas Hardy**: Macmillan Publishers Ltd and the Trustees of the Estate of Miss E. A. Dugdale. **A. E. Housman**: The Society of Authors as the literary representative of the Estate of A. E. Housman. **W. B. Yeats**: 'A Dream of Death' taken from *The Collected Poems of W. B. Yeats,* A. P. Watt Ltd., on behalf of Anne and Michael Yeats.

Prion have endeavoured to observe the legal requirements with regard to the rights of suppliers of illustrative material and would like to thank **Mary Evans Picture Library** and **Hulton Getty** for their generous assistance.